FIRE

Written by Alex Hall

ELEMENTS

Gareth Stevens
PUBLISHING

Please visit our website, www.garethstevens.com. For a free color catalog of all our high-quality books, call toll free 1-800-542-2595 or fax 1-877-542-2596.

Published in 2025 by
Gareth Stevens Publishing
2544 Clinton St.
Buffalo, NY 14224

Written by:
Alex Hall

Edited by:
Rebecca Phillips-Bartlett

Designed by:
Ker Ker Lee

Cataloging-in-Publication Data

Names: Hall, Alex.
Title: Fire / Alex Hall.
Description: Buffalo, NY : Gareth Stevens Publishing, 2025. | Series: Elements | Includes glossary and index.
Identifiers: ISBN 9781482468571 (pbk.) | ISBN 9781482468588 (library bound) | ISBN 9781482468595 (ebook)
Subjects: LCSH: Fire--Juvenile literature. | Combustion--Juvenile literature. | Four elements (Philosophy)--Juvenile literature.
Classification: LCC QD516.H355 2025 | DDC 541'.361--dc23

This edition is published by arrangement with Booklife Publishing

Printed in the United States of America

CPSIA compliance information: Batch #CW25GS: For further information contact Gareth Stevens at 1-800-542-2595.

Find us on

Photo Credits – Images are courtesy of Shutterstock.com, with thanks to Getty Images, Thinkstock Photo, and iStockphoto.

Recurring images – gravity_point, fluke samed. Cover – fluke samed, Christian Roberts-Olsen, Valentina Shilkina. 2–3 – lassedesignen. 4–5 – Peter Gudella, Mikhail Bakunovich, Mikhail Bakunovich. 6–7 – Benevolente82, zhengchengbao, Good Job, Galyna Lysenko, Ara Hovhannisyan. 8–9 – VectorMine, Milkovasa. 10–11 – JGA, Gorodenkoff. 12–13 – rangizzz, Gorodenkoff. 14–15 –Christian Roberts-Olsen, Jackal Yu. 16–17 – Audio und werbung, TFoxFoto, Chones. 18–19 – Trevor Bexon, NadyGinzburg. 20–21 – Studio Romantic, Botond Horvath, Pixel-Shot. 22–23 – Vitalina Rybakova, New Africa.

CONTENTS

Words that look like <u>this</u> can be found in the glossary on page 24.

ESSENTIAL ELEMENTS

Life on our planet would not be possible without the four elements. The elements are water, earth, fire, and air. Each element has its own important job. Together, they keep the world in balance.

These elements are essential because the world cannot work without them.

Have you ever wondered how fire starts? Fire has many different jobs on our planet. Fire can even be different colors, from yellow to blue!

Let's heat things up by looking at fire.

WHAT IS FIRE?

Fire is what is created when something burns. When something burns, it is called combustion. Fire makes heat and light. The power of this heat and light can be used in many ways.

Most matter is a solid, liquid, or gas.

Solids are firm and do not change shape easily.

Fire is none of these. Very hot fires can become something else called plasma.

Liquids flow and take the shape of the container they are in.

Gases such as air don't have a fixed shape.

THE FIRE TRIANGLE

The fire triangle shows how fire is made. Three things are needed for a fire to start. These things are oxygen, heat, and fuel. If one of these things is missing, then a fire cannot start.

Fuel is the thing that a fire burns to keep going.

Have you ever seen someone light a match? Heat is created from the movement of the match. The match itself then fuels the fire. There needs to be oxygen in the air around the match.

THE SPARKS OF LIFE

Humans have been using fire for millions of years. Early humans did not live in houses. Having fire helped them keep warm. It was also used to keep them safe from animals.

Early humans also discovered they could use fire's heat to cook food. This made many foods easier to eat. Learning to cook made humans healthier and smarter over time.

I SEE FIRE

Fire makes light. For early humans, the sun was the only source of light during the day. The discovery of fire allowed humans to see at night once the sun had gone down.

Humans used fire to make lamps. The first lamps were in rocks or shells. Humans filled them with a plant called moss and covered it with animal fat. These were then set on fire.

FOREST FIRES

A forest fire is when a large area of a forest catches on fire. Humans often accidentally start forest fires. Fires spread easily in dry forests where the plants can be used as fuel.

Forest fires can be very destructive. Fire can stop plants from ever growing back and leads to habitat loss in the area. Humans need to work together to put out huge fires.

FIGHT THE FLAMES

Fire is very hot. This means it can be dangerous. Fire can cause burns if someone gets too close. Fire makes smoke. Breathing in too much smoke can also be dangerous.

Smoke alarms tell people when smoke is in a building.

Firefighters are trained to put out fires. To put out a fire, they need to get rid of the heat, the oxygen, or the fuel. They use lots of different tools to do this.

Fire extinguishers are used to stop some fires.

TOO MUCH SMOKE

Large fires make a lot of smoke. Smoke is bad for the environment. Smoke is made up of gases that cause air pollution. Polluting is the act of putting harmful matter into the natural world.

Have you ever noticed smoke coming out of cars? Most cars work by burning fuel, which makes harmful smoke. You can help the environment by walking or biking to school or the store instead of using a car.

FUN WITH FIRE

Fire can be used safely for many activities. The candles on a birthday cake are set on fire to be blown out. Fireworks use fire to blast into the sky during celebrations.

Do you like baking? People use the heat from fire to bake goodies such as bread, cookies, and cakes in an oven. What is your favorite thing to bake?

FANTASTIC FIRE

Fire helped humans become who we are today. The discovery of fire helped people live longer and become smarter.

Fire still helps humans in their daily lives. The heat from fire is used to heat homes and cook food in ovens. How do you safely use fire in your life?

GLOSSARY

balance the state in which things exist in the correct amounts to keep things stable

destructive having to do with causing a lot of harm

environment the natural world

habitat loss when something causes a living thing to lose its home

oxygen a gas that living things need in order to survive

plasma matter somewhat like a gas that has a lot of energy in it and can conduct electricity

source where something comes from

INDEX